D0332148

Locked Up With Success

A Prison Teacher's Guide to
Closing the Achievement Gap in Any Classroom

By

Janice M. Chamberlin

ISBN: 1451552424

EAN-13: 9781451552423

NOTICE

DISCLAIMER

This book is dedicated to my dad, Bruce G. Chamberlin:
my hero, my mentor, my role model

About the Author:

Janice Chamberlin has been an educator in public and private schools, a case manager for Child Welfare, and a businesswoman. Her undergraduate and graduate degrees are from Indiana University, and her All Building Administrator License was completed at Indiana Wesleyan University. She feels her most successful and fulfilling work thus far has been as a teacher of adult male inmates. Janice further believes her experiences in the prison setting are an untapped resource for all teachers who wish to close the achievement gap. This is her first book. Ms. Chamberlin lives in Michigan City, Indiana. She is rich in friends and family, especially her grandchildren.

TABLE OF CONTENTS

Chapter 1: Welcome to My World   15

Chapter 2: Unlocking Student Potential   23

Chapter 3: Securing a Safe Setting   33

Chapter 4: The Keys to Keeping Track of
Everyone and Everything   53

Chapter 5:   Locking Up That Success   65

PREFACE

Whenever I am asked what I do for a living, there is first surprise and maybe a little bit of shock when I say I teach at an all- male prison year round.

I can almost predict what people are going to say. They'll want to know if I'm afraid. "Is there a guard in there with you? What do you teach them? How do you get them to learn?"

"I wouldn't do what you do for twice your salary," is what I'm often told.

Generally, my first response is to tell them it is the most challenging and rewarding teaching I have ever experienced. I then proceed to explain the setting and offer many stories. My dad, especially, has always said, "You should write a book."

Even my colleagues have come to me more than once and said, "What do you do that produces increasing numbers of GED's every year? What's your secret? Do you just get the 'cream of the crop'?"

Well, that has to be a joke, because teaching in a prison, I think the "cream of the crop" would be difficult to find.

In 2006, I went back to school to earn an administrative license. I learned that many of the things I had been doing all these years had been proven, by brain research, to work in teaching. Then I got really energized, because I could put into words what the success was all about and why things worked for me and for my students.

In recent years, I have been doing a bit of work in the public schools, working on an internship, doing some tutoring and assisting with after school programs. When I observed the little kids again, the light bulb just went on. I saw many of the same behaviors and lack of skills that I have seen in my adult students.

These would include things like poor decision-making skills, a lack of listening skills, a need for immediate gratification, anger issues; those kind of things.

That's when I realized I had valuable information for any teacher. Those I especially want to reach with this book include:

- Teachers who are currently teaching in a correctional setting, as well as those who may find themselves in that career in the future
- Those who teach in any other adult education programs
- Those who teach in urban schools or alternative schools, no matter the age of the students
- Teachers who work with students who have special needs

This book offers suggestions on how to maintain a well-managed, organized, disciplined and safe learning environment. You will learn how to teach creatively and successfully, while still being able to exhibit the word that we hear all the time, *accountability*.

I believe my story can help you close the achievement gap wherever it occurs, regardless of the age of the students you instruct. I think I may even have a secret or two to share.

This most challenging teaching position may hold some keys to successfully improving education, overall. I intend to give you what has worked for me.

Let me be clear! I am not in any way suggesting your students are heading for prison, or that you should treat them as "inmates." I am simply suggesting that some of my teaching methods, based on what I have observed and experienced in my classroom, could work for others.

Since 1973, I have been involved in education. I clearly understand the issues, the frustrations, and the passion of educators. Once you read about my classroom experiences and philosophies in a prison setting, I think you will be able to apply my methods to your classroom.

My experiences are an untapped resource that I believe can make a difference for you, no matter where you teach.

So, turn the page and let's begin.

1

Welcome to My World

For thirteen years, I have taught in a correctional facility, mostly teaching adult males between the ages of 18 to 75. I also have nearly a year's experience in an all-male juvenile facility, with ages ranging from 12 to 18. So, I have experience with a full spectrum of ages.

The prison setting obviously has many cultural and ethnic backgrounds. We have Caucasians, African Americans, Native Americans, Mexicans, Puerto Ricans, and probably any combination of the above.

The ability levels range from non-readers at kindergarten level, all the way to twelfth grade. Until recently, our school was departmentalized by subject area, and the students were also placed by academic level. Specifically, I taught the high-level math. These students were at the high school level; I instructed them in numbers and operations, measurement, algebra and geometry.

A couple of years back, we changed to a system of self-contained classrooms. Some of the teachers still specialize, preferring the lower or the higher academic levels, but I teach in a totally self-contained environment with all subjects: reading, writing, social studies, science, and math. And I teach all levels from kindergarten to grade twelve.

I have had students who knew their letters, but didn't know the sounds that the letters make, all the way to students who were just about ready to graduate from high school, but for one reason or another never finished.

The makeup of the academic levels is much lower than most people realize. I taught one man who never completed first grade. He said his family moved around a lot, living in the woods, so no one realized he wasn't in school. At last count, twenty three of my forty five students were under the fifth grade level! I usually have at least four or five in each session who would definitely be in special education classes if they were in the public schools today. Those four or five would have their own special education teacher. And that instructor would probably even have a teacher's aide.

Picture this setting. Three men, all in their forties and fifties, are working on their subtraction. One is very timid and toothless. One is stocky, kind, and doesn't appear slow. The third one is easily angered and has a large scar down the side of his face. All three men are under third grade ability, and they're arguing about the best way to subtract single digit numbers. The stocky man is showing the timid one how to use his fingers to figure out the answer to 7 minus 2. The guy with the scar starts an argument as to "what number comes first, the top or the bottom." If it wasn't so sad, it may have been funny watching them argue. Finally, I intervened and explained they could say "7 minus 2" or "2 from seven." The guy with the scar was happy because somehow he determined that what I told them proved he was "right." I let him think he was correct and moved on to another problem.

Our supplies, our technical equipment and our materials are quite scarce. For example, there have been times when we only received 20 pencils a month, and these were shared among 40 to 60 students each day. Someone in the bean counter's office determined that one pencil should last for 129 pages. I used to get angry, now I just chuckle and make do the best I can.

My overhead projector was last repaired in 1988, according to the ticket on it. I recently obtained a TV, VCR and DVD player. A couple months ago a whiteboard was delivered, which I have been waiting for since I started teaching at the prison.

"New" computers for us are usually several years old when we receive them. And, for security purposes, Internet access is out of the question. Basically, I have several choices of textbooks, an overhead projector, a TV monitor, a DVD/VCR player, and a few computers that are literally years old.

Another issue most teachers don't deal with "on the streets" is that I am limited in what I can bring into or out of the institution. We are shaken down at the front gate every morning; we take off our shoes, coats, and jackets. We remove everything from our pockets. Our bags and lunches are searched for contraband. We are not allowed to bring in what many people would consider basic supplemental educational materials. We can't just walk in with a book, a DVD, a magazine, extra pencils, or even a newspaper without first getting permission.

As they say, "It is what it is," and this is not to be critical. I simply want to illustrate that success can be attained, even with a lack of supplies.

Another recent change that affects our school is increased stress, because the Department of Corrections wants us to speed up our promotion and graduation rates. I know this is also the case in other schools. They want more for less: more production, better results, less money and less staff.   It's more accountability, accountability, accountability.

So what do we teach in prison? We work on adult basic education skills for those who aren't literate. The first goal is to reach 6th grade in reading, math, and language skills. Once reached, the next goal is to pass the GED test. Forty per cent of high school graduates in this country cannot pass the GED test. It's not as simple as many think. So it is a major accomplishment for a man to move up to a level that allows him to pass the test.   After the GED is passed, there are other educational opportunities, including vocational programs and Purdue University classes which can lead to certifications and degrees. Our vocational programs include classes in computers, marketing, horticulture, automobile repair, electronics, culinary arts, and construction trades. My colleagues and I are very dedicated to helping the men become contributors to society. This also lowers the possibility of them returning to prison.

The offenders do receive a time credit, sometimes known as a time cut, both for reaching literacy and/or for passing the GED test. They also receive time cuts for completing a vocational program, or for earning Purdue certificates, associate and bachelor degrees. These time credits allow them to be released as much as a year or two earlier than their original sentence. This saves the state thousands of dollars per inmate, which is another reason top administrators want more promotions and more completions.

We have what I would call the ultimate diversified, mainstream classroom. We have students with ADD, ADHD, learning disabilities, various degrees of hearing loss, depression problems, lack of sight, and epilepsy. We educate bipolar individuals, stroke victims, diabetics, and people with high blood pressure. Alcoholics and addicts are very common. Some of the men have brain damage as a result of accidents or shootings. I have taught several men with prosthetic limbs.

Lots of anger issues exist in our classrooms; most of the men are ticked off that they are even in prison. They're mad at the judge, or whoever may have turned them in, or at themselves.

There are also relationship problems. Someone is always going through a divorce.

The death of a parent or spouse causes extreme stress. When a man goes to prison, he rarely thinks about the possible pain of missing his mother's funeral. Losing custody of children, or even termination of parental rights, can be a reality. Some deal with sick or troubled children and with sibling problems, all of which cause much stress for the individual who is going through any of these traumatic situations.

And then, of course, there is the lack of control. They often can't do anything about their problems, so it's an understatement to say they come into class with a bit of anger and frustration on their plate.

Most people are surprised to hear there is no security officer assigned to each individual prison classroom. I have up to 25 individuals in each class, and I am basically responsible for the security. Occasionally, a security officer does come down the hall, or we can call for help from an in-house phone, if necessary. But basically, I discipline my own classroom. Chapter Three will elaborate on how I deal with discipline, safety and security.

The challenge is to produce more results, more quickly while still honoring our mission statement. The mission entails encouraging lifelong learning as we prepare the inmates to re-enter society as productive citizens. We are always trying to develop new strategies and to maintain high standards of teaching, as well as increasing efficiency. Sound familiar? I know that's a silly question.

It is very difficult to reward the inmates, because we can't bring anything in or do anything that would be construed as trafficking. Trafficking is defined as giving something to the offenders or taking anything of value from them. I cannot even buy pencils for my students, because that would be considered trafficking.

Once at Christmas when I was very new, I had hopes of bringing in a cookie for each of the students. I wanted to bake Christmas cookies for them but was denied because there are issues with people bringing in marijuana-laced items. Plus, it's considered trafficking to share food.

Fraternization is also not allowed. This would include any behaviors which could be construed as getting too friendly with an inmate, whether by giving them special attention or favors. If you use your imagination, you can probably realize what favors a male inmate might want, even from an older female teacher.

So, positive reinforcements are difficult, but not impossible. For example, awarding an occasional certificate, allowing them to choose a video to watch, and verbal positive comments are acceptable. However, I do have a secret weapon I will tell you about in the chapter, of all places, on organization (Chapter 4).

The conditions are poor. Temperatures get too hot or too cold. Mold and high humidity ruin the books and the sinuses. Pipes break, creating steam leaks and additional mold. Once, I was helping a man at a computer and several men called my name. I didn't turn around; instead, I told them, "Hang on a minute." They sounded agitated so I looked in their direction and realized my ceiling fan had broken loose. It was dangling about three feet from the floor, hanging by one wire, as it continued to oscillate. Thankfully, no one was hurt. One of my colleagues from down the hall assisted me by disconnecting the fan until it could be repaired. Things break down all the time, and we often wait months or years for repair. Several years after the fan incident I came upon that poor fan crammed in a storage closet. For all I know, it's still in there.

Another issue is huge student turnover. Out of up to 50 men I will typically see in a day (25 in the morning and 25 in the afternoon), I expect to gain or lose at least two or three each week. According to my records, I average 10 to 15 men leaving, and 10 to 15 men entering *every month*.

Some leave because they pass the GED test. Some simply quit. Others are moved to a different part of the facility, or to another prison, due to discipline issues. Some are sent to work release or to drug programs; some are actually released to their homes. And then, of course, new students are always starting class. So, I deal with a great deal of transition.

Essentially, we work on a year-round, circular basis. Whenever I make a presentation, some men are just coming in while others may be on their way out. This is another thing I have to consider when planning my lessons. For some, my presentations are an introduction; for others, they are a review.

Under all of these conditions, I figure if what I do works, I imagine at least something can be applied to your school environment. Accountability and doing more with less are a part of all schools; increased class sizes, little or no prep time, less supplies, less teachers, little or no professional development. Does this sound familiar?

I know it sounds a bit cheesy, but even though this is a discouraging and challenging time in U.S. education, I also believe it can be the most exciting. I have had my teacher's license since 1973, so I am not a young "Mary Poppins". I have had my share of ups and downs, and I still believe we can succeed in improving the educational system for all. It's our opportunity to make changes that will improve teaching and learning, as well as to stick to the tried and true methods that still work.

Now let's look at how to unlock student potential.

2

Unlocking Student Potential

The largest amount of my time, and probably one of the most important things I do, is creating an environment where my students *believe* they can succeed, and where they *want* to succeed. I understand those who say no one can be motivated by anyone. I understand their reasoning. However, I'm talking about setting the stage where students who are afraid to learn, or hate school, or don't believe in themselves, can feel safe and thrive in an educational setting. If that can't be accomplished, very little learning will occur.

Most of the men come in with very diverse recollections of what school was like. School wasn't cool, and they still have no use for education. Probably up to ninety percent of them despised school, and they certainly disliked authority. In my case, some of my students have an issue with a woman in an authoritative position.

Many of the younger students, and even some of the older ones, don't understand why they need a GED, why they need to learn to read, or why they need to be educated. They believe since they have always had a job or they can get a job, it won't make a difference in their life whether or not they are educated.

I spend a lot of time selling them on the value of education, what it can mean to them, why they need it, what's going on in the economy, and what advantages it will give them to go home with an education. From our school, they can also move up to vocational programs and college programs right in the facility. It doesn't end just with a GED. I am always trying to push lifelong learning.

Now when I say "sell", I don't mean simply telling them. They have to come to this conclusion on their own. It has to be sold by slowly showing them the advantages of learning. This is done through discussions, posting articles on the bulletin board, and comparing needed job skills from each of their life experiences. We refer to a wall chart which illustrates every math concept needed for each of many careers. There's always the math lesson which allows the students to compare lifetime income of non graduates, to high school graduates, and to college educated individuals. I share literature which indicates an education makes the inmates less likely to recidivate, or return to prison. Some realize they want to help their own children. And some even find value in making their parents, grandparents, spouse or children proud of them. Whatever it takes!

We have a lot of students with low self-esteem. One student I'll call Mr. Miller was really, really smart, but he just wasn't doing anything in class. It dawned on me he didn't know he was so smart.

Mr. Miller cracked me up one day when he was looking at a world map, and said to me, "I don't understand why they even label the oceans. Why do they have an Atlantic Ocean, a Pacific Ocean, and a Lake Michigan? When you're in a boat and you're just driving along, or you're in a ship and you're riding along, there are no signs out there that say what ocean it is. Who cares what it's called? Why'd they even have to name them? You just have to go across them."

I spent a little time explaining to Mr. Miller about the massive amounts of water in the world, and what it would be like if we didn't delineate the exact location of the oceans, lakes and rivers. Finally, something clicked with him and he said, "I can't believe all the shit I don't know!"

After that, he was fine and on his way to learning. He now understood there *was* a lot to learn and maybe there was value to it. And he finally believed he was capable of learning; that he was intelligent.

Mr. Miller eventually passed the GED Test; you've never seen a prouder man. "Ms. Chamberlin, if it was allowed, I'd take you to dinner because you've helped me so much! Don't worry; I'd bring my wife, too." And he smiled his toothless grin. Gratifying situations like this happen all the time.

I used to think all of the students coming in and out of my classroom had low self-esteem. But I soon realized there are some students with very high self-esteem. A cocky attitude was misinterpreted as low self-esteem. But some of the criminals actually do have high self-esteem. They have no problem with themselves and think that everything about them is simply wonderful. It baffles me, but even though a man commits a crime, he may very well have no esteem issues whatsoever.

Power struggles are frequent. Usually at the beginning, a student tries to establish his turf. He'll show a bit of "gangster mentality." He may try to act like he doesn't care. He is probably afraid, but he doesn't want anybody to know. He may be embarrassed, but doesn't want anybody to know that, either. Instead, he tries to control me and everyone in the room.

Depending on the man, sometimes I have to get stern and let him know who's in charge. I let him know he's in "my territory", or on "my block". Usually, that is the end of it, and he'll settle down. For another guy, I might give him a few days and he'll settle down on his own. Some guys just have to see how much control they can grab. It's just another issue we have to settle before learning takes place.

Another thing I do to motivate the students is to figure out the real meaning for their attitudes. It helps with motivation and with classroom behavior, which are intertwined.

Mr. Lopez was meaner than a snake. He was probably in his fifties, and he was an old curmudgeon. I could not break through to this man to get him to do any work. He didn't see the value of studying, and was snotty to me all the time.

Finally, Mr. Lopez ended up leaving school. I can't remember if I ended up throwing him out because he wasn't producing, or if he quit. But it taught me a lesson; I thought this man had a really ugly heart and was very mean-spirited. I totally misunderstood his behaviors.

At lunch one day, I was in the chow line, and Mr. Lopez was serving food. He said hello and we chit-chatted for a few seconds. Out of nowhere, Mr. Lopez said, "You know, the reason I hated school and the reason I gave you trouble was because you look like my ex-wife. She's blonde, she's short, and her name is Jan. You remind me of her too much."

We just laughed, and I was like, "Oh, for Pete's sake, that's what it was."

He never came back to school, but it did teach me a lesson; sometimes there is a reason why people act the way they do. And if you can just break through that, you usually have it made.

There was another individual with tattoos over every part of his body. Mr. Thornton was quite intelligent. One day he was sitting in class and asked for a math test. He wanted to see if he was close to being ready for the GED test. I quickly handed him one.

About five minutes later, Mr. Thornton threw the test and yelled, "Don't you *ever* give me another fuckin' test when you know I'm not ready!"

A natural reaction would be to throw him out or to holler back. But I just stood there, listened, and smiled at him. I knew he hated math, he was very low in it, he was probably afraid of failing, and he was embarrassed.

Mr. Thornton got all stressed out, so we had a visit. I acknowledged his frustration, offering to help him as often as necessary. I told him stories of the many others who hated math, were frustrated by it, but who eventually passed. I also stressed that further outbursts by him would not be tolerated. Months later, after much perseverance, Mr. Thornton passed the whole GED test, including math. He went on to take Purdue classes while still in prison, and became one of my best advocates with new students.

After he passed the test, you would have thought I was supernatural. Mr. Thornton talked to everybody about how they needed to listen to me and how great he thought I was. And he tells the story over and over about what he did in his early class days and how we butted heads a little bit, but that it all worked out in the end.

Then there are students who try to get kicked out. It reminds me of foster children who know exactly what they need to do to get kicked out of a foster home. They figure it's going to happen anyway, so they might as well get it over with. Some probably don't believe they can pass the GED Test, or are too lazy to try. If they can get kicked out by "mean Ms. Chamberlin", then they can blame me instead of themselves.

These guys, especially the younger ones, will get really angry and rude. They are often very intelligent, but they'll do whatever they can to get thrown out. So, knowing that, I visit with them, let them know I'm aware of their plan (even if they don't realize what they're doing), and usually I can get them to decide to stay and try.

I'm reminded of one young man; I'll call him Mr. Marlon. Mr. Marlon was about nineteen, was angry and hollering most days. He was very volatile, but I also could tell he was extremely intelligent, probably almost genius level.

One day while the men were in the library, as a last resort, I took Mr. Marlon out into the hall to talk with him. I took a chance and told him what I believed to be his life story. I must have hit a nerve, and was apparently very correct in my assessment of his life. He started to cry, and I was thinking, "Oh, Jan, what did you do now?"

We talked a long time and he started telling me what had happened; he had been in foster care because his dad used to hit him on his head with a rifle. Mr. Marlon wanted to stop the cycle; he had a young child himself and didn't want his son to grow up the same way he had. And he certainly didn't want his son to get into trouble, also ending up in prison.

Just by acknowledging all of that and letting him know that I understood and would try to help him, Mr. Marlon's behaviors totally changed. He calmed down, and he ended up not only passing the GED Test, he earned an "Honors GED". His scores put in him the 99th percentile nationwide. Finally, Mr. Marlon became one of my best tutors.

I never knew what happened to Mr. Marlon after he was released. I generally never know once they get out of prison. But I think something turned around that day. At least in my class, his behavior changed and he became an asset to the classroom, as well as a much more educated young man.

These examples illustrate that sometimes discipline and security are better maintained when we try to understand the reasons for the outbursts. Often, this eliminates future problems. At least it did with those individuals.

Acknowledging there is pain and anger helps immensely. I often tell them, "If you're not at least somewhat angry or depressed, I'd think something was wrong with you. If I lived here, I'd be crying every night."

Some of them admit to me they *do* cry every night, as quietly as they can, and I respond, "You're bound to be depressed, and angry at someone or something, or even at yourself. I try to make this classroom a safe haven where you can come to get away from being in prison for a few hours a day. Obviously, we have to follow some rules. But this is, hopefully, a place where you can control at least one thing. You can work on improving yourself and go home a better man. You can't control anything else in here or at home, but you can get more educated and improve your chances of a better life." This usually softens them up.

Having someone acknowledge their pain, though not allowing them to dwell on it, opens up their learning potential.

Note I said "not allowing them to dwell on it." I'm not a counselor, I'm a teacher. So I don't spend a lot of time listening to their stories, excuses, or complaints. Sometimes, it is necessary in order to assist them in getting onto the path to learning. But it's usually a matter of acknowledging their pain and getting back to work.

Trust is another big issue. It takes time for me to earn it, and it never happens automatically. They see me as the "police". They don't trust anyone, including themselves, and they will tell me that.

Sometimes I acknowledge this to them, because they think I don't understand them. I'll say, "I know you probably see me as an old lady who doesn't know anything, who's just going to give you trouble. And given a little time, you'll find out that's not true."

I try to encourage them to stick with it for at least one month. "Let's go a month at a time." Ninety percent of the time, if they stick with it, they calm down and life in the classroom is fine.

Once in awhile, I see a concrete example that this encouragement pays off. When I first met Mr. White, he exhibited very immature behaviors. He struggled academically and always wanted to quit. In fact he did quit at one point. The policy didn't allow him to return to class for at least 90 days. He did eventually return, progressing three grade levels within about a year, reaching literacy.

One lunch hour he appeared at my classroom door. Mr. White hesitated a moment, then said, "I just want to tell you thank you. In the two years I've been here, you're the only one who has helped me. You kicked me in the butt and made me work. I may not have improved much, but it's because of your help that I learned anything. I just wanted you to know you have made a difference in my life." Teachers live for conversations like that.

Another approach I find successful is the "think of me as your coach" talk. Some of these students are quite anti-establishment, which is putting it mildly. They don't like authority. They want that GED because they want to go home early. But they don't think anybody else knows how to get them to that goal. They want it now and they want to do it their way. And to a certain extent, I let them do it their way, until they start to fall on their face. Sometimes it helps to give them the old "coach talk".

I say, "Think of me as your coach or your personal trainer, and we're all practicing for the big game."

They understand that. They can relate to that pretty well. So then I say, "What if you think you should be working on dribbling the ball, and I'm telling you that you should be practicing your free throws? Do you think you're going to play the big game next week if you're over there dribbling that ball?"

And they always say, "No, no, no."

Or I'll say, "If a personal trainer told you to work on your upper body today and you said, 'No, I'm going to work on my calves,' how long would the trainer put up with you?" They get that.

All of my work in motivating sets the stage for learning, but it also serves another purpose. It leads to a more disciplined environment.

3

Securing a Safe Setting

Contrary to common belief, I am at least 90%-95% of the security in my classroom. My biggest approach can be summed up as showing an authoritative, but also a caring, demeanor. It takes a little bit of work and a bit of balance. But it works well for me and I think probably for most people, if it's done consistently. If I can overcome their poor attitudes, then discipline is obviously easier.

Often, people think since I teach adults, classroom discipline must be easier than when working with teens. In reality, many of these men are physically grown, but are still mentally equivalent to young teens. I have found by observing their behaviors, I can come pretty close to figuring out at what age they began using alcohol and/or drugs. Their achievement test scores give me the second clue. If a man comes to school at a sixth grade level, it's usually safe to say he began dabbling in alcohol or drugs around the age of 12. It helps in knowing how to approach a man, and how to develop his educational plan when I understand where he's at academically and emotionally.

The Department of Corrections places each inmate based on several factors. They are sent to any particular prison after considering the severity of their crime, the length of their sentence, and their risk of violence. The higher level security prisons house the death row inmates, for example. The lowest level prisons might not even have a fence. They house those who are determined to be the least risky or dangerous. How dangerous are my students? It varies; the prison is a medium security correctional facility. So none of my students are on death row, but I have taught drug dealers, addicts, car thieves, rapists, child molesters, murderers, and armed robbers. You name the crime, and I've probably taught someone who committed it. Am I afraid? Rarely. Do I need to be vigilant and careful? Yep.

I do my best to explain the reasons for the rules, and they are always supposed to sign them when they first enter school. We put the rules in writing and they sign, so they know what the rules are. I allow their input, but there are some rules we simply must follow because we are in a prison. I also post the rules to avoid grievances; they can't say they didn't know any particular rule. We make them as general as possible; respect for each other, follow orders, things like that.

As for obscene language, I don't allow it. And they must have their pants pulled up, their shirts tucked in and buttoned, and their ID's on their shirt pocket, but I still always explain that. I stress it's not because I am in a power struggle, or because I am trying to be the boss. I tell them, "We do this because if you go home and dress like that at your job, you're going to get fired in less than a day."

They don't always accept that, but as a general rule they do. If not, I approach it as a disciplined setting for learning; for example, in a military setting, there are rules for dress and self-discipline.

"It's a practice in self-discipline, which helps you get in the right mode for learning." They don't always buy that, but very often it does work. If you explain your reasons, it's a little harder for them to argue about it.

There are some exceptions to the general rules. Sometimes it's necessary to be more specific. I walked into a colleague's classroom a couple years ago and had to laugh, because he had a sign hanging on the wall with just two words on it. In bold print, it said, "No spitting."

I chuckled, "What is that doing there?"

He, too, chuckled and responded, "Well, I had a student who was hocking and spitting right on this floor."

When he tried to correct the student, the guy said, "Hey, there's no rule about that. Nobody said we couldn't spit."

In cases like that, you throw up a little sign. The next time the student spits, he can't say he didn't know it; at that point, he becomes subject to loss of privileges or more time to be served in the prison for not following a direct order. I think that sign is still hanging there, even though "Joe the Spitter" is probably long gone.

I have learned to be constantly observant and aware of my surroundings. If it's too quiet, for example, I had better pay attention, because something could be wrong. Any difference in the norm is cause for attention; no matter how small a change may be, you kind of perk up a little bit and watch to see what is going on. One morning, as early as 7:15 A.M., I had just thought, "Gee, it sure is unusually quiet. They're all studying nicely, but it almost makes me nervous." Within seconds, I heard a loud banging sound. I looked up to see one guy standing over another, pounding the stuffing out of him. I phoned for assistance; the "cavalry" showed up, threw on the cuffs and dragged the two guys out by their feet. The damage was minimal. I cleaned up the blood (using universal precautions, of course), and the guys simply went back to work. But the incident woke me up that morning, to say the least!

They are never all terrible, but there are usually several in a class that will try to pull something. Mr. Pierce was always coming in 10 to 15 minutes for the afternoon sessions. I had been teasing him about always being late and wondering why this kept happening. I was suspicious he was up to "no good" but I didn't mention it to him. Mr. Pierce was always saying he had to clean his room, and I was responding, "That doesn't make sense, because everybody else is showing up on time, and they've cleaned their rooms."

I eventually said, "You know, you're kind of making me start to wonder if you're involved in something, if you're selling something or sneaking a cigarette somewhere." He kind of chuckled, and I laughed. But believe me; I had my eye on ol' Mr. Pierce.

About two days later, I got a call from a security officer who said, "Would you send Mr. Pierce up to his dorm immediately?"

I looked at the class, realized Mr. Pierce was gone and said, "The Officers are looking for Mr. Pierce. Where is he?" They said he was in the bathroom, but several were laughing. I thought it was strange they would laugh simply because he was in the bathroom.

I saw one of my other students, suddenly acting like he had to go to the bathroom. He took off and went down the hall. I speculated he was going to warn Mr. Pierce of something.

I didn't say a word and acted very calm. I picked up Mr. Pierce's books and said to the students, "I'm going to take his books down to him. That way, if he doesn't make it back to class this afternoon, he will still have his books for studying in the dorm over the weekend." They chuckled again, so then I *knew* something was up.

I stood outside of the bathroom, and I waited and I waited. I called to see if Mr. Pierce was in there, and he answered. Suddenly, I realized he had flushed the toilet three, four, five times. That's when it dawned on me that he most likely had some type of contraband and was trying to flush it. At that point, I called for a couple of officers; they went in and retrieved Mr. Pierce.

After class, two officers came to my room and thanked me. Sure enough, Mr. Pierce was trying to flush a cell phone down the toilet; cell phones are a big "no-no" in prisons. I was the heroine of the day, and Mr. Pierce is no longer in our institution. He was shipped to a higher security level because of the cell phone.

Again, this illustrates how small things can matter. It's not like I am constantly suspicious of everybody, but when you observe enough, you start to sense when an incident is about to occur.

Another thing I find about discipline and keeping the classroom safe is to stay as calm as possible. It seems some students feel it is their job to stress out the teacher. That's how they "win" for the day. This was very apparent when I taught in the juvenile facility. I was called more names in the first ten minutes on my first day than I have been called in all my years teaching the adult inmates. The juveniles were also expert at leaving little drawings on my desk. These usually involved cartoons of me and one of the inmates. I won't go into detail, except to say they were shockingly pornographic and insulting to me. One day, a similar drawing was drawn with pencil, three feet high, on the back wall of the classroom. After the classes were dismissed, I simply handed the drawings to the officer on duty, and cleaned the wall myself. Because I didn't go berserk or scream or cry, the juveniles didn't know what to do. Eventually, the name calling and shenanigans slowed down. I'd be lying if I said they totally stopped. But they never saw me get upset over it. I was only "on loan" at that location for a little under a year. If I had continued there, I believe the classroom environment would have improved even more.

Some students like to steal things, so you have to be careful. They want the littlest things you wouldn't even think people would want. I basically have to guard everything.

They will try to take transparent tape by wrapping a bunch around their pencil. They love to take paper, especially colored paper. I think they like to make cards to send home, but they still can't be allowed to steal things. Paper clips are a hot item; they can be used as a variety of little tools or even in making weapons. They love markers and colored pens. The ink is used for tattooing, so it's kind of a big deal if they obtain those.

An electric pencil sharpener will be stolen for its motor. They will take any kind of plugs and motors, and use them to make tattoo guns. The men are absolutely ingenious as to what they can build. Things that you would never even think of as being a valuable item, they'll steal. You can't let them take anything, because it could be a security issue later on in the dorm. Any piece of metal can be turned into a weapon. Since the men don't have much, while in prison they'll pay for anything imaginable. If a guy can steal wanted items, he can make a small fortune.

They might steal in order to sell things to other inmates, even though selling any item is against the rules. Possessing anything of value can lead to fights, blackmail, and all kinds of other issues. You have to watch every man and every item, just to maintain your small amount of supplies.

It is prudent to trust the students as much as possible, but it is also prudent not to trust any of them, even if they appear perfectly well-behaved. There have been many incidents, where the ones that were very quiet and I thought were the "perfect" students, were the ones actually stealing. Their plan is to build up my trust. Once they think I'm not suspicious of them, they think it is "safe" to take advantage of the situation and slide out a set of headphones, a couple calculators, or a box of pencils. Oh, and I can't forget about batteries. Remote controls are easy prey for a couple AA batteries.

I don't fear the inmates' intimidation, and I don't usually fall for their manipulations. However, once in awhile I have been known to get duped. I remember Mr. North, who acted really innocent and sensitive. I cringe now when I recall how I tried to help him get medical care. He would cry, and tell me disturbing stories how the nurse would yell at him and not let him see a doctor. I went out on a limb, making phone calls to advocate for him. After three or four times of helping him with various issues, I started to finally catch on to his manipulations. Boy, did I fall for his garbage! Soon after his release, I read about him in the national news. He had been incarcerated in another state, subsequently escaping, terrorizing and robbing all over the country. By the time he was apprehended, he was charged with the rapes and murders of two women; he now sits on death row. Mr. North had apparently manipulated at least one other staff member while he was in our prison. That woman became romantically involved with him and actually helped Mr. North obtain weapons. To this day, when I think about Mr. North I wince. He sat in my classroom as a student, then as a tutor for nearly a year. I tried to help him because he had a sincere, pathetic manner. I definitely misjudged Mr. North. He taught me to be alert to manipulation.

When it comes to discipline, consistency is the name of the game. I can't stress enough we have to be consistent in all we do. If the students don't know what is expected of them from one day to the next, they become frustrated. They'll also be more likely to cause trouble. If they know the consequences, and that they will be held accountable in a fair and predictable manner, behaviors will be less troublesome in the long run.

I used consistency when raising my own children. I used it when I was teaching in the public and the private schools. I have had very good luck with running a consistent, predictable program. There are days when I feel tired and don't want to be consistent, but it is really important to stick with the plan. I've learned the hard way when I get lazy and don't follow up on consequences, control is eventually lost. If I should allow even two or three men to be late for school without at least a warning, the others become angry and defensive. They watch everything I do and throw it back at me if they even *think* someone else received preferential treatment. Before long, they accuse me of a lack of fairness and discrimination. Valuable class time is lost and stress levels rise for all concerned.

In all schools where I have taught, consistency amongst teachers could be lacking, too. Students pick up on teachers who are not consistent from one classroom to the next. The more everyone can work as a team, the better the environment for the students and the teachers.

Kindness can coexist with consistency. I believe the steadier and more reliable you are, the more flexible you can be. Students respect consistency and fairness and, as a result, are more likely to accept rules. Little room is left for arguments. So when an occasional accommodation is necessary for another individual, the others are less likely to make a big deal about it, because they know the particular situation is rare. They know that I must have a good reason to do something a little differently.

The specific approach that has always worked well for me is progressive discipline. I start with a verbal warning and I plainly tell the student, "I'm giving you a verbal warning. You know that you're supposed to be on time but you're ten minutes late. I'll cut you some slack this one time and just give you a verbal warning." Usually, they thank me for not putting anything in writing. And generally, it doesn't happen again. I document the incident by jotting a little note on the attendance chart next to their name.

The next step would be what we call a corrective notice. This is a written warning. It doesn't cause them any trouble, and it doesn't lose them any prison days or any good time. The student signs, indicating he is aware of this rule; he knows he broke it, and additional occurrences could lead to what we call a conduct report, dismissal from school, or both. If he refuses to sign, I simply check the box marked "refused to sign."

The final step, if rules continue to be broken, is the actual conduct report. This can lead to consequences imposed by the prison. It's rare to get to this point, but it must be done when necessary. If not, the consistency goes down the drain, and control can be lost.

Document, Document, Document! That's always been my mantra. It has worked well for me. If they should file a grievance, or if somebody questions why I made a student leave school, I have documentation. If the students know what is expected, and they know the consequence(s) for not complying, it is easier on everybody. I know it's not a new idea, but I think it merits reviewing, because we tend to fall away from it. And once we fall away from the consistency, we have to re-establish control. In the long run, that's more work than simply following the progressive discipline plan.

A frequent expression in my classroom is, "It's all about choices." If they bring in a mug with naked ladies taped all over the sides, they have decided to break a rule. If they made the choice, then it is on them if they have to suffer the consequence. It is not on me, and I don't allow them to put it on me. We don't have to fuss and scream about it. We don't have to argue about it. It is simple. It is very quiet. It is very peaceful. All I do is write it down, they sign, and then we move on.

If I said nothing ever goes wrong, I'd be lying. If I said these guys never get on my nerves, I'd be lying, too. Sometimes I just want to scream! They can remind me of "mosquitoes." There are times when I can't walk down the hall to go to the bathroom without several guys stopping me for one reason or another. As one of my favorite officers once said to me, "Sometimes I hate these guys! Nothing's worse than a bunch of grown men acting like little bitches"! Of course, the men didn't hear his comment, and I wouldn't have worded it exactly that way. But he sure hit the nail on the head. The trick is not letting them know they're getting to me, and to stick with the plan. It's on those days it's imperative to stay calm, smile, and remember to stay consistent.

Sometimes, though rarely, I have had to discern what is best for a student and haven chosen not to follow up with progressive discipline. This is an example of the room for flexibility that I referred to earlier. One afternoon a student, Mr. Thomas, was acting really agitated and angry. I have taught enough special needs students to wonder if perhaps he was supposed to be on some type of medication. He was exhibiting what appeared to me as manic behavior.

The first problem was how to approach Mr. Thomas without asking too many personal questions. I took him into the hall so we could speak privately. By the way, that is always a classroom joke. I'll say to a student, "Step into my office," and he'll walk out into the hall. That way, not everybody hears the discussion, because things can easily escalate if they all hear what is transpiring. Also, they usually cooperate better with me when they don't have an audience.

After a few minutes he stated he was bipolar and only takes his medications when he needs them. The ethical problem for me came when he told me he stores his pills up, and he had enough to overdose if he wanted to.

I knew the prison's rules against an inmate having any prescription medications in his cell. It is always dangerous, and I was worried he was storing them up, maybe for suicidal purposes. The more likely possibility was he was selling them to another inmate which is a serious offense. Another concern was if I reported him, the other students or Mr. Thomas might later accuse me of "ratting" him out. That put me in a precarious situation.

After thinking about all of this for a few minutes, I decided the most pressing issue was the possibility of a suicide plan by Mr. Thomas. He had mentioned his brother had committed suicide which heightened my concern. I didn't relay my thoughts to the student, but I was concerned he might have been contemplating suicide, which is a much larger concern than if he was selling the pills. I asked his permission to call the psychiatrist on his behalf. He was skeptical the doctor could help him, but he agreed to let me make the call.

Rather than get him in legal trouble and, therefore, also getting him expelled from school, I decided the ethical thing to do was to call the psychiatrist. I immediately did so, and his office sent Mr. Thomas a pass for an emergency appointment.

I was never told the results of the appointment, but Mr. Thomas came back to school the next week, and he seemed much better. His behaviors were more leveled out.

Unfortunately, about two months later, Mr. Thomas again became very disruptive in my class, exhibiting behaviors indicating he either wasn't taking his meds, or he needed them adjusted. This time, he was uncooperative with me so I sent him back to his cell for the rest of the day.

I immediately went to the Director of Education and showed him my notes from the past month. We decided to have Mr. Thomas searched. He had six pills on him. Since then, he was moved to a different teacher. It wasn't safe to keep him in my classroom, as he suspected my role in his "shakedown," and he was upset with me. I never heard if he received any disciplinary consequences, but I may have stopped him from hurting himself.

Sometimes one has to look at a situation and quickly discern what is best for the individual student, what is best for the classroom, and thirdly, what is best for one's self. In that case, I thought the best option was first to try and help Mr. Thomas. When that didn't work, we had to go ahead and confiscate his pills and move him out of my classroom.

Another rule in prisons, though I know it has become more of an issue in all schools, is "no touching is the best policy". It is a prison rule all inmates know, and it can lead to a write-up for them. They cannot touch any of the staff.

Occasionally, I have given a professional handshake. When a man is on his way to be released and he is thanking me for helping him pass his GED, or he is thanking me for being his teacher, or coming to say goodbye, I will shake his hand.

No one wants to do anything that could be misconstrued as battery, or some kind of sexual proposal, so we just don't want to touch.

Drawing, sketching or doodling in class seems fairly benign but is another discipline issue. It may simply seem to be a distraction when students are supposed to be studying. But often, they are working on "gang" symbols, and/or they are designing tattoos. So it needs to be stopped.

"Gangs" is a term we don't really use anymore. We call them S.T.G.'s. I always thought that sounded like a sexual disease, but it stands for "Security Threat Groups." Gangs are out. Security Threat Groups are in.

There is much to learn about gangs, but I am not going to address it at length here, because it is a security issue. We don't publicize a lot of what we know. My advice here is to make sure you keep up on what is going on in your neighborhood gangs, so you recognize the signs of a gang showing up in your classroom or in your school. Gangs exist everywhere, whether anyone admits it or not.

The symbols they draw, the way they wear their clothes, the hand signs they "throw" change all the time. Whatever I might write today about S.T.G.'s will be different by the time this book is published.

You will be trained and updated about gangs in any prison or jail in which you teach. And you will have seminars in your schools to keep you updated on gangs. You should always try not to ignore the fact that Security Threat Groups exist; trust me, they exist.

It's either funny or pathetic to envision, but flirting happens quite often. I think some of the men are actually hoping for sexual favors from me, even though I could almost be their grandmother. Trust me, if they could get away with it that is where they would go with it. A female teacher could be 300 pounds, have all kinds of zits on her face and be 92 years-old, and they would still flirt with her, because there aren't too many females around. But, usually, the main reason is they are trying to manipulate, to soften up, or to charm. They will make little comments like, "Those earrings are really pretty, Ms. Chamberlin." "Your hair is really 'new school'." "That color looks great on you." "You look like you're no more than 35 or 40." Seriously! They say silly things like that!

I think many of the men probably mean well, and aren't actually flirting. But many of them *are* trying to soften me up, and I have my standard responses. I'll say, "Son, you've been in prison too long." Or, "Son, $0.65 a day doesn't do it for me." That tends to give them the hint to back off.

Usually, it is the younger ones who are doing this. It isn't the old men flirting; they are usually a bit more respectful. It tends to be the younger ones who think they can receive some kind of favor. Maybe they want a better grade, or to get away with something in class. Or they hope I won't notice they are stealing, or whatever it is they have on their agenda.

They are always trying to get information. They will ask, "Are you married? Do you have kids? How many? Where are they? Where do you live? What kind of car do you have?"

One student said, "Do you smoke?"

I said, "No."

He said, "Does your husband smoke?"

I didn't tell him I didn't have a husband but instead responded, "No, and I'm not bringing you any cigarettes."

He looked at me really funny, because he realized I knew what he was trying to do. He wanted to see if he could get me to bring him in some cigarettes. One cigarette can be sold for up to $6.00, so inmates often fish for clues that a staff member is interested in making a little extra cash. Eventually, they will catch on as to who won't cooperate with their shenanigans.

You just don't give them any personal information. You can be kind, but I usually say, "You know I don't give out that information," or, "That's kind of personal." Sometimes it takes a blunt, "That's none of your business."

You have to be careful, because they are always looking for information. They work among themselves to try and piece it all together. The next move would be to look for ways to "get over" on a staff member for one thing or another. For example, if they can get the sense someone might be hurting financially, then that person would be more likely to bring them a cigarette, or sneak them in some food, a cell phone, or some pills in exchange for cash.

But if you even give them a piece of candy, look out. If you give them something one time, then they have you, and they can blackmail you further. It has happened to numerous people. It is a very slippery slope, and you do not want to go there. When they're done blackmailing you, they'll report you to the authorities.

Discipline is for everyone's safety. It is not simply a power struggle. On the surface some things seem picky but, realistically, could be very dangerous. Tell the students why, for example, they need to be on time. I tell them, "I'm responsible for your safety. To you, I may appear overly strict, but you could be getting beat up in a stairwell somewhere, and no one would even know to look for you." That usually disarms them and softens them a little bit.

Another tactic students often try is raising their voice and saying, "You can't talk to me that way!" Or they will say, "I'm an adult. You can't talk to me like I'm a kid!"

I have heard that many times, and I have learned to calmly respond to those comments. I don't have to scream back at them. I just say, "Sir, I know how you're talked to on the dorms. I know how other inmates talk to you. I haven't used profanity. I'm not saying anything disrespectful. I'm just asking you to sit down."

Or I'll tell them, "Ironically, you want me to talk to you like a child, rather than like an adult. Because when I tell you what you need to hear, or I'm upfront with you, or "real" with you, you don't want to hear it. So you accuse me of talking to you like you're a little kid. If you *were* a little kid, I would say, 'Okay honey, that's all right. That's okay. You can do whatever.' And I'd be really sweet and very grandmother-like to you. That's treating you like a child, which is what you want me to do." Again, that kind of disarms them, and then they are usually okay.

One thing we as teachers can never forget is humor. You have to joke around sometimes. You can tease gently, but you cannot make fun of them. I never make fun of my students for not knowing anything academically, or for when they do something that is socially unacceptable, but there are ways you can kindly tease them.

Every spring the seagulls come home. We're fairly close to one of the Great Lakes, but the gulls come to hang out at the prison's landfill. We subtly comment the chow hall will soon be serving more chicken. "And those chickens sure seem small to me." The looks on the guys' faces are priceless.

We also know it is spring when we can have the men look out the window, and introduce them to Mr. Possum and Woodrow E. Chuck, our resident pets.

Sometimes they will use incorrect grammar, saying 'He bee's funny,' and I'll joke with them about it. And then, maybe five or ten minutes later, I will comment that, "I bee's ready to collect the calculators". They will reply, "Oh, Ms. C's got jokes," and everybody laughs. It makes it a little more pleasant environment if we have fun.

I'm going to go out on a limb and tell you about a day when I *did* tease a student inappropriately. Mr. Cunningham was barely twenty years old, and had only been in my class for about three weeks, so I didn't know him very well. Class had only been in session for a few minutes one morning, when he referred to me as "Ms. Loaner." I didn't respond until about the third time he said this because I didn't even realize he was talking to me. In big black letters, "LOANER" is written in several places on each book. It eventually dawned on me and the others that Mr. Cunningham thought my name was "Ms. Loaner"! I have to say we all laughed, and I TRULY thought the man was playing a joke on me. However,

I'm embarrassed to say I shot back with, "You're either as dumb as a box of rocks, or you missed your calling as a great comedian!" Ouch! You should have seen the poor guy's face. He gave me a blank stare, then a mortified look. I about crawled under my desk with shame. I truly thought he was kidding when I made the comment. But as soon as it came out of my mouth, I saw he was NOT trying to be funny. I apologized profusely, but I'm not sure he understood. So here's the lesson. Watch what you say, especially when a student is new and you don't know him well. I did know he was at a low level academically. But I didn't know how low, and I hadn't yet figured out he was also emotionally handicapped. As I observed the poor guy over the following days, I became concerned and decided to write to my supervisor and the security supervisors about him. I was worried that another inmate might hurt him or take advantage of him, and I was hoping they would keep an eye on him. I still don't know quite what his diagnosis was, and he's since been released from prison. But I sure learned my lesson about opening my big mouth before thinking. I probably hurt his feelings, and if I'd have made the comment to the wrong guy, I could have put myself in danger. That wasn't one of my finer moments.

Another frequent comment I make to my students is, "We play, but we don't play," and they know what I mean by that. We goof around, we enjoy ourselves, we have a nice time, but we work hard learning. There is a limit to playing, a line they cannot cross.

As mentioned previously, I strive to create an environment that caters to their various needs for learning, as well as to create a safe and supportive learning environment. We have all heard this before, but it is worth reminding ourselves; if they feel safer emotionally, they will enjoy school. And if they are happy and feel supported, more learning will take place.

This type of environment also helps in lowering discipline problems. Discipline problems make for unsafe and unsupportive environments. Everything must be done to offer safety for the students, as well as for the staff.

Obviously, once in a while we have to call on law enforcement or on security officers for assistance. But good instructional practices, motivational techniques, and consistently enforced discipline policies are some of the pieces that help with safety for all.

Finally, develop relationships with security staff, case managers, medical and psychiatric staff, all the support staff, and with any other stake holders in your building and your community. Collaboration improves cooperation among everybody. When all parties have good relationships, information flows more freely. That helps everybody to assist the students. And in the long run, it also improves security.

Next, let's take a look at how to keep track of everything and everyone, better known as classroom management.

4

The Keys to Keeping Track of Everyone
And Everything

One of my biggest successes has been in my ability to organize and develop good classroom management. I believe we all have it in us, to an extent, but some are better than others. I think it is a learned skill. I also believe if you are organized, you can afford to be more flexible.

That seems like somewhat of a backward thought. It would seem the more organized a person is, the more rigid he or she would be. But the more you have everything in order, and the more you know where everything is, the more flexible you can be when something you have to deal with pops up out of the blue. I find myself less stressed and more able to be flexible, when there is a system in place.

Administrative edicts have made it imperative to improve results, and this is probably true wherever anyone teaches. Teachers are mandated to be more accountable and more efficient, as we are expected to individualize each student's plan and to differentiate their assessments. I have developed a plan to help accomplish that. In addition to educating students more quickly, it is important to me that we continue to provide a solid educational plan, rather than just a little learning factory or GED factory. So, I set up some criteria to determine the direction I wanted to go.

I decided my plan had to cover the academic standards needed to reach literacy or to pass the GED test. It had to be flexible and it had to be individualized. It needed to be simple to set up and simple to administer. It must give each student control of his plan. It can easily be duplicated by other teachers, if they want to borrow it or use it. And it would maximize the production of every student.

Over a period of years, I developed progress sheets for each of the five subjects: math, writing, reading, science, and social studies. These are for every level, and for every subject. I probably have 35-40 progress sheets I use regularly. For every text used in my classroom, I created an Excel program on my computer, where I made a chart with all the assignments, all the page numbers, a place to put their name, date, score, and some notes at the bottom. Whenever I need one for an individual, I can just print it out quickly and we're good to go.

I used to keep these student records in my own files, but now I have created a folder for each student to keep. In his folder, I put any sheets that will help him track his daily progress, and to track his assessment results. I also include learning aids and charts, a goals calendar, etc.

When a student enters my class, he is taught the logistics of the plan. This is a crucial step in the process as he is going through his orientation. Many students need assistance with their folders. They have difficulty organizing, setting goals and recording their progress, so

I start teaching these skills as soon as they walk in the door.

They need to know they are responsible for their own learning. So, I teach each student to take a pretest for each subject and how to determine which assignment he needs to complete, based on the pretest results. Then the tutors or I take those charts I have made, and show him how to color in which assignments he determines he needs to do.

This is not easy for a lot of students, but once you get them to understand the pattern, in the long run it saves everybody a lot of time and a lot of grief. Everybody knows "who is on first", so to speak, and it clears the way for educating.

They are also given supplemental materials such as calculators and rulers. They're offered all types of supplemental books they may borrow. A student can study his materials when he is not in class, which also speeds up his progress. When in the classroom, he can also choose to watch videos or complete appropriate computer programs, in lieu of the core books. That helps to address different learning preferences and styles.

Prior to entering class, achievement tests established each student's approximate grade level abilities in reading, math, and language. So the classroom pretests simply hone in more clearly on exactly what skills need work, and what skills have already been mastered.

Each student now has his own individualized plan with his own input. He will know exactly what he needs to accomplish. He can work at his own level for each individual subject and have *control* over how and when to do this. If he is poor in math, he might spend most of his mornings working on math, and then a smaller amount of time working on his strengths. He can balance out his abilities, and each student usually enjoys having something he can control. He will have power over his time, and the ability to work on what subjects and skills he chooses during any given session.

Each student grades his own daily work, keeps his own records, listens to the required lectures, and marks them off on his checklist once he completes them. He writes his required essays, and he decides when he is ready to take the GED practice test. This allows more time for the teacher to assist the students directly, to periodically monitor their progress, to critique essays, and to prepare for small and large group presentations.

It also creates more time to work with the lower level students, who generally need much more direction and instruction. The lower students, the third and fourth graders, and even the kindergarteners use this system, but they have *much* more direction and guidance, depending on their abilities.

Now, here's the motivational secret I spoke about earlier. In a prison setting, concrete rewards are really not allowed. But I have learned rewards and punishment can *lessen* the chance of self-motivation, and *appreciation of learning is its own reward!*

Setting goals and having control over them is an alternative to using rewards! It increases the student's *self-motivation*. If a classroom offers choices in learning that demonstrate mutual respect, it is a supportive learning environment for the students, and they are more likely to self-motivate. In the long range scheme of things, isn't that what we ultimately want for our students? Ironically, in an environment where I can offer little or no rewards, my students can learn to motivate *themselves* which is inherently a much more desired trait than reacting to any outside rewards or punishments.

To further support the success of my students, I help them develop planning calendars, set goals for their work, and establish criteria for quality. They learn to pick dates for goals and monitor their progress along the way. And then, together, we make changes in their plans whenever it is deemed necessary. We tweak and discuss their plan whenever we meet. There are certain things they know they must do. There is no option as to *what* they have to learn, but there may be options as to *how* they learn it.

We practice the art of mastery learning. Sometimes my students have a little difficulty with grading their own work, because in their mind they think it is cheating. So, I take time and explain there is another way to learn. When they have completed a couple of questions, if they are not sure, they can look them up, stop before they make a lot of mistakes, and fix them before they go any further. Then, they can use me as a resource if they don't understand what they are doing wrong.

It does take patience and some time, but the system is all in place. I have tutors who set up a lot of this for the students in advance, because we know when they are coming in as new class members.

If doing all of this produces more GED graduates at a quicker pace, then I have accomplished my goal. The bonus is it helps to self-motivate. I don't have to worry so much about always pumping them up and telling them how great they are. Don't get me wrong. I compliment them as much as possible. I have a personal goal to say something nice to each student at least once a day. There is great value in that. But I can't give them M&M's, or a little cookie, or a free pencil, or any kind of concrete reward. So, my system is a more practical and effective replacement.

Basically, I have little or no preparation time. In my official schedule, I have 15 minutes a day of preparation time for 40 to 50 students. And they each have their own individual education plan that I just outlined for you. So, my organization plan is absolutely crucial, even if all it does is save me valuable time.

Again, consistency is imperative. It takes hard work, constant engagement, observation, analyzing, tweaking, and an awareness of the surroundings. But if you create a system for yourself, for any tutors or clerks or student teachers you might have, and for the students, it is going to pay off big time. Stress levels will lower, productivity will increase, your students' academic levels will increase, and you'll be able to illustrate this concretely to your administrators.

As for tutors, I use inmate tutors. I generally use two in the morning and two in the afternoon. They do clerical work for me, make student folders, grade pretests, fill out assignment sheets, and/or help teach the students how to manage their own plans.

Also, the tutors explain operations and procedures to the new students. They help with daily work, at a student's request. They keep books and supplies in order and accounted for, and they sign out books students wish to borrow.

I choose tutors based on their trustworthiness, and their respect of the other students. I don't tolerate arrogance from them; they must treat the students as equals. I also appreciate self-starters. They must have a lot of initiative.

I don't care whether or not tutors have a college degree. Some of my best tutors are former students who passed the GED Test. By the time they've earned their GED, they already know the organizational system and the way we work. And if they are good at working with the other students without making them feel embarrassed, then that student is potentially a great tutor!

It takes time to train tutors, but in the long run it is very, very worth it, because they help immensely.

Let's talk a little bit about collecting information and data. We all have been made to do it more often in recent years. I enjoy it and have always done it. Data offers a way for me to see changes that need to be made, and where I can improve. When we stop looking for ways to improve, that's when we get stale, when students start losing interest, and learning is not happening like it should. So try to stay very fresh.

I don't keep statistics in order to be a boring person who's a numbers freak. Rather, I actively analyze those numbers. Obviously, I have to collect them for the administration, but I also like to use them for my own improvement.

For example, one July I tested approximately 50 students. I was looking for grade level ability. It was also an achievement test to see who had improved. If I had asked the students or other teachers what would be the lowest scores, most would have hypothesized math. To my surprise, over 70% of them were either deficient or not improving in language!

So, I used this data to determine most, if not all, of the men needed extra help in language arts. Even the highest level students were below sixth grade. I was shocked! My challenge was to figure out a way to improve the language ability of this many men with a wide range of grade levels. In this case, it was grades one through six. I looked further through the results and saw even the most intelligent men simply did not know basic grammar rules.

How could I continue to use individual educational plans, and still help so many different levels with their language?

I began developing plans which would incorporate many academic and interest levels. The goal was simple. I would provide at least one lesson each day as a small or large group activity. I made a list of necessary concepts centering on grammar, punctuation, and writing.

I advised the men of my plan, and they seemed anxious to participate. They even gave me ideas on how I could pull together as many of our limited resources as possible. Sometimes we worked in pairs or teams, sometimes as a whole class. Those who were low level readers or writers would work with those who were stronger. New students arrived almost weekly, which meant we also had to think about a circular approach; each new lesson was either an introduction for some or a review for others.

I provided several practice worksheets for each lesson, and they were able to choose those that were the most comfortable for them. They worked on some in class and took some to the dorms over the weekends. We found lessons on our computers and in various levels of texts for each concept. They practiced writing on the overhead projector, on large sheets of paper, and on the chalkboard.

This was a unique experience for them, even though it was archaic by most standards. But they loved to help each other. They enjoyed writing their sentences and paragraphs on the board. We had contests for the most creative and the funniest. Prizes had to be make-believe or verbal, since you can't bring such things into the prison. We had a little awards ceremony, honoring the "Sentence Structure Specialist", the "Grammar Guru", and the "Prince of Punctuation".

Three months later, when I re-administered the tests in October, I measured quite a bit of success. We had set the goal for everybody to improve by six months, but an average of a two-year improvement was what we actually obtained. That was quite reasonable, because some of the students are able to learn quickly; they just were never exposed to the material. That was a big growth in just three months. I was very pleased, as were they. They knew how much they had grown and were as happy as clams.

I also use my statistical data to develop my own goals. When we can look back and see what we did, then we can predict. I always know my numbers, so I can predict growth for the next year and figure out how I want to improve.

In my self-contained classroom, I did a compilation of 180 students I taught over a three-and one-half-year period. Of those 180 students who came through my classroom, 66 passed the GED exam. When I subtracted out those who were removed because of discipline issues, went home before they could get their GED, or quit, 75% of my students passed the GED test.

My average numbers can tell me how to predict my results for the following year. I know that for every group of men that I send to the Practice Test (the official Practice Test is administered by another staff member to determine readiness for the GED), 75% will pass. Of those who pass the Practice Test, 90% to 95% will pass the GED.

To some people, that doesn't mean anything, but to me it is really important, because then I can make predictions based on how many students I have, no matter what their level. Over the years it has worked out quite consistently, so I can make predictions as to what I will do the following year.

I use those records for accountability and to show progress, or lack thereof, and to help improve my teaching. Where am I strong? Where am I weak? And, of course, these numbers are entered into monthly and quarterly reports to administrators.

I have come to believe many federal, state and local mandates meant to improve the educational system are full of political rhetoric. Most teachers have probably come to similar conclusions. However, I also believe good teaching can be a science, and that there is always room for improvement.

Keeping score, whether for myself or for mandated reports, is how I know if students are improving. Even though I believe many of the testing mandates, for example, can be misguided and sometimes outright ridiculous, I am glad to see closing the achievement gap has been brought to the front burner. These mandates have created chaos and frustration, but also more dialogue in the whole country. And, to me, that is very exciting, because whether or not we like the accountability/measurement issues, it really can improve our production.

Education today is more challenging than ever, especially when I am under the mandates of the Department of Corrections, as well as the Department of Education. I have learned when faced with adverse and difficult policies and mandates, there are two types of educational leaders: those who allow the culture they are building to disintegrate, and those who view opportunities to add creative value to their school.

We need to close the achievement gap, and those who are succeeding at adding creative value *are* closing that gap!

If you are interested in receiving samples of forms for your organizational system, or in sharing ideas in this area, go to www.lockedupwithsuccess.com .

5

Locking Up That Success

These are the best of times for me, because in all my years of teaching I have always attempted to measure my success as a teacher. I am happy to see "science" has been added to the "art" of teaching, and I believe the two can be combined nicely.

In this chapter, I want to talk about how we unlock all of that success. After motivating the students, providing a safe disciplinary environment, and organizing the classroom, we get down to the "meat" of our purpose. I'll offer scenarios and anecdotes of things that have worked for me.

Thirty years ago we may have used different jargon, but many of those teaching methods still work. Due to brain research we know scientifically *why* some methods work better than others. We know we need to differentiate and to offer tiered assessments. We know we have to work more with technology and concentrate on the mastery of learning.

For example, most teachers have had the more advanced students read to the lower readers, or work on fractions with them. We believed it helped both students. Now, it's called peer teaching and we know that teaching others is one of the best ways to learn. We've taught students to compare and contrast; now we know it's at the top of the list when it comes to important learning skills. It has become easier to prepare lessons based on what is *known* to work, rather than simply trial and error.

Measurement skills can be efficiently tested with tiered assessments. I had never heard the term "tiered assessment" until recently. That's one of those methods I have used over the years but now find there's a new, "official" name for it. Many of my students have a very difficult time with measurements, so the goal was for all to learn to measure with accuracy to a quarter-inch. They were given a chart pre-developed by me, listing ten items in the room that were to be measured. They were offered a choice of three ways to complete the assignment.

I set out all the necessary materials, and posted instructions for three different ways to demonstrate at least 80% mastery. One choice was to simply measure the ten items to the nearest quarter of an inch, and then to write those measurements next to each item on their answer sheet. The second option was to make a chart themselves, and record their measurements. The third choice was to make a scale drawing, to place the measurements on the scale drawing, and to orally describe the results to the class.

That last option allowed them to use colored pencils, and you would have thought I gave them the moon!

The smartest man in the room chose the easiest assignment. And that's okay, although it annoyed me that he took the easy way out. I can't say he was lazy, though, because he got it done really fast, and then completed a social studies assignment he wanted to finish.

Every other man picked the hardest assignment. I think part of it was because they take pride in picking a more difficult task. I also think they liked the idea of working as a team, of having colored pencils and drawing out the picture. Some of them were from a construction background, so it was their way of showing their skills. I try to highlight their strengths and skills whenever possible.

It takes a lot of work, but once lesson plans and assessments are developed, I merely hang on to them. As I have mentioned, I can use them at other times, because six or eight months later, I have almost entirely new students.

I have no choice but to honor diversity and to individualize instruction. It is an understatement to say I have vast diversity in my classroom. I teach twelve months out of the year, but the students flow in and out on a weekly basis. Several students leave, and several enter each month. There are set standards of what needs to be mastered, but each student is on an individual plan and on an individual schedule.

I have had students who never finished first grade and some who nearly finished high school. Some grew up in foster care, some were molested, some were wealthy and on drugs. The ages range from 18 to 75. I once had a student who was blind. Many have learning disabilities, and a great number suffer from mental illness. I even experienced a man having a stroke during class. So, it is definitely a challenge to meet all their needs.

Once their readiness levels are established, we develop a plan for each student. Contrary to common belief, we do have a curriculum; we don't just randomly choose what to do each day. Good recordkeeping is a must, as are frequent individual meetings to assess progress. I spend much time speaking with each individual student, learning his likes and dislikes, his background. Then, whether I am instructing an individual or a group, I can frequently go back to something they are already familiar with, and relate it to the new information being presented. I can refer to a man's carpentry job, his teenage daughter, his basketball skills, his knowledge of motorcycles, or his love of cooking. One of my lowest level readers loved anything related to speed; muscle cars, hydraulic roller coasters, things like that. Together, we planned reading and math lessons with his interests in mind.

I make a conscious effort to tell them what I am doing and to teach them to do the same thing for themselves. For example, I guide them in relating percentages and fractions to money. Everyone understands money. When they see the relationship between cents and percents, they understand the similarities among fractions, decimals, and percents almost immediately. Most of the guys have never made the connection between fractions, percents, and the names of our coins. I can practically watch the light bulb go on when a man realizes that a twenty five cent coin is called a "quarter" because it is one-fourth, or a quarter of a dollar. They grin as they then comment, "Oh, so three quarters makes seventy five cents. I never realized that. That's SO easy!" This makes them feel successful and encourages them to further pursue learning math.

I have also tried to promote a positive environment, showing them success they didn't believe was possible for them. A large share of my challenge is getting a student to believe he can learn. Once he realizes that, great things begin to happen.

In our prison, all disabled and special needs students are mainstreamed into the classroom. Individual education plan conferences and case reviews tend to be sporadic, and sometimes don't happen because of the age factor. Legally, if they are over twenty-three, we don't have to provide the special services we must offer the younger individuals. If they are under twenty-three, by law we have to provide all of these meetings.

Generally, it is up to the individual teacher to accommodate each student. The best way to explain this is to give a personal example.

In April 2006, I received a request from a gentleman who was 100% blind, to be enrolled in school. The immediate reaction was a bit of fear by anybody I approached with the request. No one, including my supervisor, thought we could accommodate the man's situation. I thought, though, we had a legal and ethical obligation to offer him services.

I obtained my supervisor's permission to interview Mr. Edwards, in order to assess the situation and see if there was anything we could do for him. I established Mr. Edwards had been sighted from birth to age nineteen; a gunshot to his face totally destroyed his vision. He had completed the tenth grade and seemed very eager to learn Braille and to earn his GED. My reaction was, "Holy cow, what am I going to do?"

I accepted Mr. Edwards into my classroom and did extensive research so I could help him. I contacted the state library, obtained a GED program on tape, a tape recorder, and made arrangements for him to sign out talking books and magazines on a regular basis.

I located an NCA accredited school, the Hadley School for the Blind. Mr. Edwards was enrolled in correspondence Braille classes. This free school is an excellent resource for anybody who has issues with blindness or poor sight. It even offers courses for people who work with the blind, such as a parent.

A special education teacher eventually provided us with a conference and made arrangements for Mr. Edwards to take the GED orally. Obtaining a talking calculator and a talking dictionary, along with a few other pieces of helpful equipment, was quite a challenge. Eventually, we got them, and he was allowed to take them back and forth to the dorm so he could study when not in school.

I accumulated three files of forms and documentation, attempting to serve Mr. Edward's needs. The red tape involved was overwhelming, to say the least. I spent time speaking to the dorm officers and to the prison case managers. Permission was obtained for him to have a key lock rather than a combination lock. He was eventually allowed to carry his tapes, cassette recorder and materials back and forth.

For the first two weeks, Mr. Edwards was in a wheelchair, so I thought he had a dual disability. I wondered if he had been shot in his spine. I didn't know quite what the situation was, but one day, by accident, I realized he could stand up. I expressed surprise when I walked in the room and saw him standing. He laughed and said, "They make me sit in this wheelchair. Another inmate was assigned to push me over to school, because they're afraid I'm going to fall. I think they're afraid I'd sue."

I'm sure the prison officers meant well. They were trying to accommodate him and make sure he was safe, he didn't fall, and nothing happened to him. But

Mr. Edwards was frustrated. He lamented that he already had one disability and really didn't need to be sitting in a wheelchair.

We worked it out. We obtained a cane for the blind through the Lion's Club. And instead of an inmate pushing Mr. Edwards to school in the wheelchair, I convinced the security staff it would be fine if the "wheel chair pusher" walked next to him, guided him to school, and nobody would sue them.

When the administration understood how important it was for the man to be able to walk and not feel like he had another disability, they gladly went along with it. It just took somebody to advocate for Mr. Edwards.

We called the man "blind guy." It wasn't meant as a "put down". It was just a joke, and he even referred to himself by the term. An administrator from the state had once been in my classroom and said, "Can I meet the blind guy?" My response was, "Do you mean Mr. Edwards?" Once, Mr. Edwards needed to write a letter to that same state administrator. He signed his letter with, "Blind Guy."

When other teachers would see him in the hall, they would say, "Hey, blind guy." "Blind guy" knew all the teachers by voice and would always say "Hi", calling each teacher by name. He was very intelligent and worked very, very hard. It took him about a year, but Mr. Edwards ended up passing the GED test, scoring very high. I was amazed, to tell you the truth. It's beyond me how a man can "write" an essay by dictation. He couldn't see, but he would tell the tester where to put each punctuation mark. He was an amazing individual!

He even learned to type. I learned more from Mr. Edwards than he learned from me, that's for sure!

The situation taught me we need to be proactive. It is very easy for disabled students like Mr. Edwards to get lost in the shuffle. We need to constantly follow up on our recommendations and be certain all people with special needs get every opportunity available to them. It was very time-consuming and sometimes a frustrating process, but it was very rewarding when I saw the progress and appreciation from Mr. Edwards.

Scenarios are another excellent way to help students learn skills and apply them to everyday life. Especially in our vocational program, we use scenarios quite often. Horticulture is learned in a greenhouse environment. Those students also care for the lawn and gardens surrounding the school. Small electronics are learned by working on broken microwave ovens, televisions and radios. The electronics teacher has a collaborative project with Goodwill Industries. The Goodwill truck delivers broken donations to the prison; the students learn as they repair the toasters, VCR's, radios and, blenders. Goodwill then is able to sell the repaired items rather than throw them away. Culinary arts students prepare luncheons. The automotive students repair and service staff members' cars. The students in Construction Trades assist with repairs throughout the institution, build custom furniture, and work on projects for Habitat for Humanity.

The challenge for most teachers is to create scenarios and maintain high levels of instruction. It takes a lot of energy and time to plan and carry out the activities. Security and time issues make it even more challenging for our prison school.

Science is an excellent example. Animals are not allowed for biology classes. Chemicals are not to be brought in, not to mention any sort of tools.

Tools are allowed for some vocational programs, but lack of time makes scenarios difficult. Even though scenarios are used very often, they must be short and simple. Only certain tools are approved, and much class time is taken signing the tools in and signing them out.

In my classrooms I use a lot of movies and videos. Many teachers I have seen will use a movie as kind of a break, or because it's easy. I find it takes much more planning for me when I show a movie, but I see a lot of positive results. The biggest challenge is getting the men to understand it is important to learn things, other than what is in textbooks. The first comment I will hear is, "I just want to get my GED." It's hard for them to understand they can enjoy themselves and learn at the same time. I explain to them everything I do has a purpose, and I have been doing this a long time. As their coach, I am saying they need a break from the books, and they will learn a lot by watching the movie or video. I try to show a movie at least once a month. It gives their brains a rest. The non-readers feel more equal, and they can sometimes shine over the readers. In this chapter I'll discuss several of my lesson plans using movies. If you're interested in more of these plans, contact me at www.lockedupwithsuccess.com .

I had an older non-reader who ran circles around the other guys when it came to history. I would show a video about a war. He knew what was coming before it came on the screen, and he was very proud of himself. The other men respected him for that, and it gave him a chance to shine.

One of the movies I have shown occasionally is Titanic. I would have thought by now everybody has seen Titanic. But as I tell my students, a lot of them have "lived under rocks." They don't go to movies unless it is a "guy" movie, a big adventure film with high action. I spend a lot of time explaining to them they need to expand their horizons. Most eventually learn whenever I show a movie, they all love it and know I am not going to give them something that will put them to sleep.

I have been doing this for years and have shown Titanic many times. First, I always have to convince them it isn't a girl movie. I work in a little bit of geography, having the men trace the path of the Titanic. We look on the map, locating where everything occurred. Then we have some discussions of the social rules at that time, the history of the ship, how it was built, and how the celebrities of the time were the wealthy people.

We read books on it, and sometimes I read to them. Pictures and a replica newspaper of the time are placed on a table for their perusal. I bring in pictures of the actors and of the real people who were involved. We analyze the cause of the sinking, and they write essays on various aspects of the history.

During one Titanic lesson, I observed an example of a student's lower level thinking, and of his lack of processing skills. At the time, I thought if I ever wrote a book, I would have to include his story in my book. I had asked the questions, "Why is the Titanic story so popular? Why does it interest so many people? Why are we still talking about this after all these years? What was historically important about the Titanic?"

A gentleman raised his hand. He was probably in his forties and very low-functioning. He said, "The Titanic brought over the Statue of Liberty."

Now, he was serious, and I had to be careful not to tease him. He said he saw it in the movie, and there was no changing his mind. We discussed it a bit more, and finally I asked, "Well, where did you see this in the movie?"

It dawned on me there was a scene where the survivors were rescued by a second ship. As the United States was finally in sight, somebody exclaimed, "The Statue of Liberty! The Statue of Liberty!"

The way the scene was shot, you could see the Statue of Liberty in the distance. But this man thought the statue was sitting on the front of the ship.

One of the other students said, "Do you think they brought it over like a big hood ornament?"

Everybody laughed without making fun of the man. It was one of those humorous times, and a good illustration of how you never know what people are thinking. Just when you think things are explained clearly, somebody processes it in a totally different way.

Another skill where my students are weak is the ability to show and identify similarities and differences. The educational literature indicates you need to be able to compare and contrast. I explain this to the men and tell them how important the ability is, and we have had lessons to work on those skills.

For example, I have shown all three movies in the trilogy Sarah, Plain and Tall. We have read the books and watched the movies, and the students loved it! I used these movies to guide them on how to compare and contrast. I did a whole lesson on how 1909 was like

2009, and how the times were different. How were the clothes different? How were the marriages different or how were they the same? I put up big sheets of paper and gave them markers, and they went up and filled in the charts.

It was very educational for me to watch this, because it was hard for them to think about it, let alone have the nerve to actually stand up and write words in front of their fellow students. Once they got the hang of it, there was no stopping them. One man contrasted the roofing. Another compared the clothing. It was a really exciting lesson. I am always bringing up compare and contrast, compare and contrast. "How is it like something you already know?"

I want to mention again how much the students love the Sara, Plain and Tall movie as well as its sequels. Never be afraid to offer a variety of movies and books. Sometimes they surprise themselves with how much they enjoy them. More than once, my students have cried over a movie that I've shown them. They even want to see some of them over and over. I believe they relate to the universal themes in some of my choices. By the way, after every movie, I ask them to list what universal themes were present. I never miss a chance to teach a literary term.

We have all heard of peer teaching in small groups, in pairs, and in whole classes. Peer teaching is a natural approach in my diverse setting. It is not always the higher level students teaching the lower level students. Sometimes the non-reader might be really excellent in math. He can then shine by helping a lower level math student, and the one who struggles in math can help the first student with word problems. What's important to remember is the one doing the teaching is learning as much as the one being helped.

There are tons of mutually beneficial combinations. Many teams form naturally, based on who they choose to work with and where they feel the most comfortable. Remember the three guys helping each other learn to subtract in Chapter One? That's a perfect example.

One of my lowest level students, Mr. Ramirez, knew a technique to better understand measurements and fractions. This was like a "Kodak moment" for me, and with a little prodding, he explained it to the whole class.

It was a hands-on activity. Mr. Ramirez had them all take a piece of paper, fold it in half, quarters, eighths and sixteenths, and then they all labeled the folds, creating an enlarged inch. I was amazed at his ability to explain this, and honestly shocked at the value of this simple lesson. Even the supposedly higher level students were clearly engaged and learning.

It is important to be on the lookout for opportunities like that. Mr. Ramirez came back in the afternoon and presented the lesson to that class. The look of pride on his face was priceless. It was also precious to see how successful the exercise was with the other students.

I find it is difficult for my students to make presentations to the class. They are more uncomfortable than most people, when it comes to speaking to groups. If a man can show just three or four others what he knows, I think that can be effective, or, at least the first step. Eventually, he may be able to teach the whole class like Mr. Ramirez with his measurement lesson.

Soft skills and the social graces, as I call them, are very important to our school. We are always working and incorporating soft skills and social graces into the lessons. Every day I never fail to mention something about manners, and proper attire. I may, on any given day, discuss speaking to groups, working as a team, or practicing listening skills. We discuss parenting skills and computer proficiencies such as keyboarding, word processing and spreadsheet creation. I encourage them to practice on the computer to become familiar with its possibilities.

Lifelong learning and the love of learning are illustrated in current events discussions, and in magazine articles I tear out and show them. John Steinbeck is an author that I like to present. We had recently watched the movie Of Mice and Men. We discussed his writing style, his biography, and how popular he was in his generation. Coincidentally, I found Steinbeck's original obituary which had been cut out of a newspaper and stuck in a library book. So, I made copies for all the students. A month or so later, a student had taken the practice test for the GED. He returned and exclaimed, "Ms. Chamberlin! Ms. Chamberlin! There was a passage on the test written by John Steinbeck!"

He was all excited and, of course, I was excited because I believe he was able to connect to what he already knew. He probably understood the passage better and most likely scored stronger on that section of the test because he was already familiar with John Steinbeck.

Another student brought in an article to share about Somalia. A couple of weeks before, I had shown a documentary about that country. We had discussed what happened in Mogadishu, Somalia during President

Clinton's administration, and what the conditions are in that country now. The student spotted an article, and I would bet my last dollar he never would have read it if we hadn't had the discussion.

Still another student brought in an article about a daughter of the Titanic casualty. He said, "I never would have noticed this, if we hadn't been talking about it last week."

Sometimes they can't read, but they will bring in an article because they saw a picture that gave them the clue it was related to what we had discussed.

I bring up current events once or twice a week. We talk about, and make a chart on, "What do you know that's going on in the world, the country, the state, the city?" They are very weak in paying attention, and need to keep up so they are not like Rip Van Winkle when they are released. And I tell them that. It teaches them government, civics, geography, science, and critical thinking skills. And it creates good essay topics for them to practice their writing.

So, always stay engaged. Tell them what you are doing and why you are doing it. Tell them they need to practice at least 21 times if they want to remember a skill. Remind them if they can hook onto something they already know, they are more likely to remember it.

We even get involved in social services. Martin Luther King Day is also the National Day of Community Service. I came up with an idea of having a food drive for a local food bank. They looked at me like I was nuts. But when I finished telling them about my idea, they decided they liked it. They realized there are people worse off than they are. Who would have guessed it, but these prisoners took on this project, and ran with it!

It was quite a sales job on my part, but once they were convinced they wanted to have a food drive, it was a treat to watch. It taught them compassion and selflessness. They organized and worked as a team. They formed committees, planned and publicized it. They made posters and walked the halls collecting items, even from the non-students.

About four hundred inmates lived in the building. The students approached each and every one of them, as well as staff members. They were strategic in who they would send down the hall to collect items. They knew who would be able to get the most from the other men.

We collected 305 items that were purchased from the commissary. The majority was their staple commissary food, Ramen Noodles, but they really did an outstanding job!

Every night I would take home as many items as I could carry. We only collected food items for a couple weeks. Then I contacted some teens from the local Boys and Girls Club who could drive. They picked up all the collected items and delivered the boxes to the Salvation Army food bank. Obviously, my students couldn't make the delivery. So the prisoners learned how to organize and complete a fundraiser; they were able to contribute to the hungry, and they even collaborated with another agency in order to accomplish their goal. Everybody was happy and it was quite the success!

It is possible to creatively educate on an individual basis, to close the achievement gap, to enjoy the process, and still be accountable. Is it easy? Heck, no. It takes constant evaluation, adjustment, and passion.

If inmates of every race, culture, economic status and education level can show measurable improvement, so can your students!

Epilogue:

A Tribute to Correctional Educators

Ironically, as this book was being edited, all the prison educators in my state were told our services will no longer be needed. We have become victims of the economy and the current trend of "restructuring". I will not make any lengthy comments here as to what I think about this decision. I'm obviously not pleased, but "it is what it is".

I wish to pay tribute to prison teachers everywhere, especially my long time colleagues. My experiences are not unique. Prison teachers are a dedicated bunch and have many stories of their own. Their experience, energy, and expertise in closing achievement gaps are truly an untapped resource.

My hope is that visionary educational leaders will consider correctional teachers when strategizing as to how to add value to their school communities. These teachers would serve well in any number of capacities; administrator, teacher, mentor, or consultant.

Made in the USA
Charleston, SC
23 May 2010